Friedrich Nietzsche
In Plain and Simple English

BookCaps™ Study Guides
www.bookcaps.com

CW00801773

Table of Contents

Introduction: Brief Biography

Friedrich Wilhelm Nietzsche was born on October 15, 1844, in a German village named Röcken bei Lützen. He was named after the Prussian king at the time, Friedrich Wilhelm IV.

Before Nietzsche turned five years old, his father died of a brain ailment; Nietzsche's younger brother died six months later. His family moved, and he spent the rest of his childhood with his mother, grandmother, aunts, and younger sister. Being the only male in a house full of women quite likely had an impact on his future philosophy.

Somewhat ironically, given his later beliefs, Nietzsche entered college as a theology and philology student—though he would soon become exclusively interested in philology, the study of historical language. Arguably his interest in philosophy started when he discovered Arthur Schopenhauer's *The World as Will and Representation*, whose high aesthetic sense combined with an atheistic worldview may very well have influenced Nietzsche's own thoughts in those regards.

In those days, Prussia required every able-bodied male to undertake military service, and Nietzsche was assigned to a horse artillery regiment when he was 23. However, his chest was seriously injured in a riding accident. At 25, he became a hospital attendant during the Franco-Prussian War, where he acquired more medical problems. Nietzsche continued to be in poor health for the rest of his life.

Possibly the most significant relationship in Nietzsche's life was the quasi-father/son friendship he shared with the famous opera composer—and anti-Semite hero of the Nazis—Richard Wagner. Nietzsche had admired Wagner's work for years before they met, and Nietzsche once wrote that the days he spent with Wagner were the best of his life. Nietzsche held a great deal of admiration for Wagner, both as an artist and, at first, as a thinker. However, as Nietzsche grew older and his views developed, he slowly began to realize that he and Wagner shared some fundamental differences after all. This can be seen most clearly in Nietzsche's book *The Case of Wagner*, written in 1888, where Nietzsche absolutely tore into both Wagner's music and his ideology, including the anti-Semitism that Nietzsche himself abhorred. It goes without saying that Nietzsche's disillusionment with his friend, hero, and probable father-figure must have had a huge impact on him.

When he was 24, Nietzsche became a professor of philology at the University of Basel, Switzerland—one of their youngest classics professors ever. His first book, *The Birth of Tragedy*, was mainly about philology; however, it came under heavy attack by his fellow philologists, and Nietzsche soon found himself somewhat alone in his profession. He continued teaching and writing books, with a more and more philosophical bent, until his health finally deteriorated to the extent that he was forced to leave his job at the age of 34.

By this time, Nietzsche was stateless, having given up his German citizenship years before—partly because he was a professor at a Swiss university and partly to liberate himself from ties to the birth country with which he had a turbulent relationship. He spent the next several years, until 1889, in a wandering existence, travelling between various great European cities. This was the time when he wrote most of the works for which he is now famous, writing a book (or a major section of a book) every year until 1888, his final year of lucidity, when he wrote five.

Nietzsche fell in love at least once, with a young Russian philosophy and theology student named Lou von Salome (despite the first name, she was female). However, Salome did not return his feelings, and their friendship soon came to an end.

Nietzsche wrote his last book, *Nietzsche contra Wagner*, at the end of 1888. While his physical and mental health had been on a decline for a long time, on January 3, 1889, Nietzsche finally suffered a complete mental collapse. According to one story, when he witnessed a horse being whipped by a coachman, he ran up and threw his arms around the animal in an attempt to save it, then collapsed. Whether this actually happened or not, however, is unknown.

He was brought to a psychiatric clinic in Basel, but they were unable to cure him. His mother took him back home in 1890, where she cared for him the next seven years until her death. In 1893, his sister Elisabeth returned home, and after reading her brother's work, slowly took control of them and their publication. Elisabeth is thus responsible for much of her brother's future renown—and infamy, for she was a Nazi herself and did the best she could to shoehorn Nietzsche's philosophy into an ideology he himself had unequivocally rejected.

In any case, his mother died in 1897, after which Elisabeth took custody of him. Nietzsche himself died only a few years later, on August 25, 1900. He was not yet 56 years old. He is buried next to his mother and his sister in the graveyard beside his family's church in his hometown, Röcken bei Lützen.

#   #   #

Before going into detail about Nietzsche's thought, it would be useful to make a few clarifying notes about interpretation.

There are many obstacles to interpreting Nietzsche's philosophy. First of all, he wrote a great many books, and they're not entirely consistent with each other. Second, Nietzsche rarely laid out clear philosophical arguments as such; he was more fond of the aphorism, or pithy quote. That makes him very quotable, but it also makes it very hard to clarify what exactly his arguments and positions were.

Because of those and other factors, there have been and are many different interpretations of Nietzsche in the more than one hundred years after his death. As long as you keep in mind that nothing said in this article is uncontroversial, though, you should be fine.

Chapter 1: Nietzsche and Nazism

Likely the most damaging misconception about Nietzsche's work has been the idea that it represented a form of proto-Nazism. Indeed, this misinterpretation was widespread even in academia, and ensured that few philosophers—at least English-language philosophers—talked about him for decades until it was cleared up. So before starting on a serious investigation of Nietzsche's thought, it would be a good idea to address the origins of the attempts to conflate Nietzsche and Nazism and then demonstrate this conflation is wrong.

As stated in the previous section, Nietzsche's sister Elizabeth was a Nazi, as was her husband. She was also the one who took custody of his work after his madness and death, as well as publishing and publicizing them. She spent a great deal of effort convincing the leaders of the Nazi movement that her brother was an ideological predecessor to them. And to a great extent, she was successful: the top Nazi "theorists" generally accepted Nietzsche as one of their own, and the Nazi regime even encouraged the citizenry to read some of his works.

Admittedly, some of Nietzsche's philosophy is easier to adapt to Nazism than others. He often speaks admiringly of power, strength, and battle, cardinal virtues of the Nazi ideology. His famous concept of the Übermensch can also be somewhat easily misinterpreted to be referring to a "master race" of sorts. (The actual meaning of the Übermensch will be discussed in a later section.) The Nazis also noted with approval Nietzsche's friendship with Richard Wagner, who is infamous for his anti-Semitism.

However, any attempt to cast Nietzsche as a proto-Nazi must ignore his several statements of contempt for both anti-Semitism and Nazism. Here are some examples of the former:

From *Beyond Good and Evil*:

> I also do not like these latest speculators in idealism, the anti-Semites, who today roll their eyes in a Christian-Aryan-bourgeois manner and exhaust one's patience by trying to rouse up all the horned-beast elements in the people by a brazen abuse of the cheapest of all agitators' tricks

From the draft of a letter to his sister:

> After I read the name Zarathustra in the anti-Semitic *Correspondence* my forbearance came to an end. I am now in a position of *emergency defense* against your spouse's Party. These accursed anti-Semite deformities *shall not* sully my ideal!!

And then there's this, again from *Beyond Good and Evil*:

The Jews, however, are beyond any doubt the strongest, toughest, and purest race now living in Europe That the Jews, if they wanted it—or if they were forced into it, which seems to be what the anti-Semites want—could even now have preponderance, indeed quite literally mastery over Europe, that is certain; that they are not working and planning for that is equally certain.

Nietzsche did not oppose anti-Semitism out of noble anti-racist sentiments, it is true. It might be more accurate to say that he despised it because of his personal dislike of its espousers, their blatantly populist appeals to the German masses. Besides, he plainly did not agree with it.

As for nationalism, this quote should suffice to illustrate Nietzsche's views on the matter, from *The Gay Science*:

No, we do not love humanity; but on the other hand we are not nearly "German" enough, in the sense in which the word "German" is constantly being used nowadays, to advocate nationalism and race hatred . . . . We who are homeless are too manifold and mixed racially and in our descent, being "modern men", and consequently do not feel tempted to participate in the mendacious racial self-admiration and racial indecency that parades in Germany today as a sign of a German way of thinking and that is doubly false and obscene among the people of the "historical sense".

It should be repeated that Nietzsche gave up his German citizenship when he was in Switzerland. Again, Nietzsche was no egalitarian democrat—he was almost the exact opposite, as we shall see later. But he saw nothing whatsoever admirable in the anti-Semitism and ethnic nationalism that even then was plaguing Germany and, to a large extent, all of Europe. If anything, he saw it as a continuation of every historical trend he hated, in particular the mass movements of people to whom he tended to refer as "the rabble" or "the herd".

The extent to which Nietzsche held these ideologies in contempt can be seen in the end of his relationship with Richard Wagner. Though Wagner was probably the best friend Nietzsche ever had, Nietzsche wrote not one but two books—*The Case of Wagner* and *Nietzsche Contra Wagner*—that essentially tore apart everything the man stood for. As opposed to his earlier works where he praised Wagner's music, in both of the above works he gave them heavy critiques. In *Nietzsche Contra Wagner*, the last book he wrote that he intended to be published, he even wrote that Wagner "had condescended step by step to everything I despise—even to anti-Semitism." While Wagner's anti-Semitism wasn't the only reason Nietzsche cut off ties with him (he was not a fan of Wagner's conversion to Christianity, for example), it certainly played a part.

To state it again, none of this is to cast Nietzsche as a grand proponent of racial harmony, although it must be said that he did support the unification of Europe in *Beyond Good and Evil*. But if one reads all of Nietzsche's works with an unbiased eye, it is impossible to conclude that he would have supported the Nazis. Quite the contrary, it is more likely he would have been one of their most vociferous denouncers.

Before going into detail about Nietzsche's thought, it would be useful to make a few clarifying notes about interpretation.

There are many obstacles to interpreting Nietzsche's philosophy. First of all, he wrote a great many books, and they're not entirely consistent with each other. Second, Nietzsche rarely laid out clear philosophical arguments as such; he was fonder of the aphorism, or pithy quote. That makes him very quotable, but it also makes it very hard to clarify what exactly his arguments and positions were.

Because of those and other factors, there have been and are many different interpretations of Nietzsche in the 100+ years after his death. As long as you keep in mind that nothing said in this article is definitive, though, you should be fine.

Chapter 2: Nietzsche on Morality

In *Ecce Homo*, Nietzsche quipped that he was on a "campaign against morality". However, in light of his other writings, especially *On the Genealogy of Morals* but also *Beyond Good and Evil*, it's safe to say that he didn't mean that seriously. Nietzsche wasn't against morality in general; he was against what he saw to be the dominant morality of European culture in his day, the "slave morality" born from Judaism and propagated by Christianity.

What was this "slave morality"? In *The Genealogy of Morals*, as the title implies, Nietzsche gave what he took to be an account of the origins of moral discourse. According to Nietzsche, the terms "good" and "bad" arose as part of the discourse of the aristocrats in ancient times, terms that described a "master morality." Essentially, according to Nietzsche, master morality called everything noble "good" and everything ignoble "bad." Of course, the aristocrats considered themselves to be noble and the lower classes to be ignoble, so morality was a way of clarifying what set them "above" everyone else. As evidence to back this view up, Nietzsche argued that the very word "good", in various languages, is derived from words meaning "noble", "aristocratic", etc.; "bad", on the other hand, he said was derived from words meaning "common", "plain", "vulgar", or the like.

So what precise qualities did the ancient aristocrats declare to be "noble"? Basically, they were the typical warrior virtues. The warrior-aristocrats valued health, strength, and honor above all else. So part of nobility was being respectful to other aristocrats and fighting honorably. But war was also valued in and of itself, as a way to make oneself stronger, and so were arguably less cruel pursuits such as hunting and dancing.

But Nietzsche's thoughts on the master morality cannot truly be described by just listing a bunch of qualities. What Nietzsche admired in master morality—though he's careful not to state unequivocally that he prefers it to slave morality, a topic we'll come back to later—was how individualistic and self-affirming it was. The nobles valued everything that came from "strong, free, happy action" (p. 11). Of course, these actions often involved oppressing and dominating the many peasants under your rule, but, as computer scientists say, that wasn't a *bug*, it was a *feature*. The aristocrats proved how superior they were by doing whatever they wanted to those who were inferior. They built themselves up by tearing others down. In Nietzsche's view, they admitted this and were proud of it. There are no "greatest good for the greatest number" calculations in master morality.

Of course, while this arrangement was certainly good for the aristocrats, it didn't exactly make the vast numbers of peasants particularly happy. It was from the oppressed that Nietzsche says we got the concepts of "good" and "evil," which characterize slave morality.

Slave morality was specifically constructed to be the exact opposite of master morality. As master morality asserted that the powerful were good, slave morality asserted that the powerless were good. Master morality gloried in strength, beauty, and privilege; slave morality built up the weak, the ugly, the poor. Slave morality damned power and everything it brought with it. Slave morality began, essentially, as the hatred of the powerful. Historically speaking, Nietzsche asserted that slave morality was invented by the Jews, before its crown was taken up by the Christians, who then proceeded to spread it to all the corners of Europe. Even the vaunted love of Jesus, he says, really grew out of this fundamental hatred of the strong.

"So what?" one might say. "Even if slave morality is based on hate, isn't it still better than master morality?" Nietzsche's chief problem with slave morality, though, is that it defines itself only in contrast to master morality. Master morality springs from self-admiration: "We are strong, powerful, beautiful, and noble, and therefore everything we do is good!" Slave morality, on the other hand, springs from contempt for another: "The ones who dominate us are strong, powerful, beautiful, and noble, and therefore everything they do is bad!" Master morality, Nietzsche claims comes out of the dynamism and excitement of life; slave morality, on the other hand, is a base kind of *ressentiment*, the projection of one's own sense of weakness and inferiority onto another. The aristocrat may kill, surely, but he does not hate: indeed, his only true enemy is one he respects, and even the peasants he crushes under his feet he can hold a kind of affection for. Slave morality cannot function without hatred. Master morality is active, while slave morality is *re*active.

So from all this, might it be concluded that Nietzsche wanted to see slave morality get eradicated and replaced with master morality? Indeed, he could be interpreted in that fashion. As Nietzsche himself pointed out, the title of one of his books is *Beyond Good and Evil* (slave morality), not *Beyond Good and **Bad*** (master morality). So perhaps it's fair to throw Nietzsche in with the other defenders of aristocracy against democracy and call it a day.

But it might not be that simple, either. Even as he criticizes slave morality, he also harbors a sort of admiration for it. And even as he defends master morality, he points out some of its faults. He notes that history was made far more interesting by the purveyors of "good and evil", while the believers of "good and bad" often held very mistaken beliefs about the weak and powerless beings to which they stood in such direct contrast. It could be argued that Nietzsche was being intentionally polemic because he believed that modern Europe was thoroughly steeped with slave morality, and in order to "wake it up", so to speak, he couldn't compromise in his description of it.

Later on, we will talk about the Übermensch, the man who creates his own values. Nietzsche's notions of the Übermensch are certainly evocative of some aspects of master morality—but it doesn't perfectly match it, either. It's not unreasonable to suppose that Nietzsche was opposed to *both* master *and* slave morality, and ultimately wanted to see some totally new system of values take its place. But that is a discussion that must await its proper place.

Chapter 3: Nietzsche on Nihilism – The Death of God

"God is dead." Out of all of Nietzsche's aphorisms, that is by far the most famous (often followed by having God humorously say "Nietzsche is dead" in response). This is usually taken to be a statement of atheism. But on reflection, this seems implausible—after all, if God is dead, that surely means that God *used* to exist, which is not what atheists believe (setting aside for the moment the question of how God could die in the first place). Nevertheless, that's the popular understanding.

Popular imagination also has it that Nietzsche is a proponent of nihilism, an opponent of meaning and morality and an advocate of pure self-interest. However, as it turns out, both of these views are misconceptions. Nietzsche did say "God is dead," but it wasn't a statement of atheism (though he was almost certainly an atheist)—and if there's one thing Nietzsche was *not*, it was a nihilistic egoist, as we think of them today.

The first book of Nietzsche's that "God is dead" appears in is *The Gay Science*, though its later appearance in the much better known *Thus Spoke Zarathustra* is likely responsible for popularizing the phrase. Here's the section in *The Gay Science* from which it's taken (translated by Walter Kauffman):

God is dead. God remains dead. And we have killed him. How shall we comfort ourselves, the murderers of all murderers? . . . . Is not the greatness of this deed too great for us? Must we ourselves not become gods simply to appear worthy of it?

It could be said that the truly important sentence here is not "God is dead," but "And we have killed him." What did Nietzsche mean by this?

Recall from the previous section Nietzsche's views on slave morality and how Christianity had propagated it throughout Europe. But in Nietzsche's eyes, the force of Christianity as a source for morality was quickly losing its grip in his day. Nietzsche wasn't the only one who thought this; many European intellectuals in the 19th century thought that Christianity was collapsing and atheism was taking its place, though their reactions to that prospect naturally varied widely. "God" in the section above does not actually refer to God Himself; rather, it's a stand-in for Christianity, or more specifically, Christianity as a system that gave people values. As far as Nietzsche was concerned, Christianity as a moral system was dead, even if Christianity as a set of ritualistic practices limped on. And it was "us", the Christians themselves, who killed it, by losing sight of the system of values at its core.

As stated earlier, Nietzsche is not the only one who thought this, and he knew that. A common conclusion to this train of thought is that, if God isn't real and Christianity is a lie, then there is no such thing as morality, values, or meaning and the world becomes empty—in short, nihilism. This is the camp that Nietzsche is often shoved into. But at the very least, it is a huge oversimplification.

Essentially, Nietzsche agreed that with the downfall of Christianity, Europe lost its source of *objective* meaning and *objective* value. But that doesn't mean it lost its source for *any and all* meaning or value. Indeed, at one point in *The Will to Power* (a collection of manuscripts Nietzsche hadn't originally intended to publish), he points out that nihilism often turns self-contradictory:

> A nihilist is a man who judges of the world as it is that it ought *not* to be, and of the world as it ought to be that it does not exist. According to this view, our existence (action, suffering, willing, feeling) has no meaning: the pathos of "in vain" is the nihilists' pathos—at the same time, as pathos, an inconsistency on the part of the nihilists.

In other words, a true nihilist would be indifferent to the fact of meaningless, as that fact in and of itself is meaningless; however, nihilists tend to express themselves in "pathos", in depression, thus implying that they don't *actually* value nothing, they don't *actually* find the universe bereft of meaning.

Nietzsche's response to the death of God is not to retreat into the false despair of nihilism, and it's certainly not to claim that the only thing important is doing whatever is advantageous to oneself. Rather, in the death of God, he sees both danger and opportunity—danger, because without an objective source of values humans might degenerate into the kind of passive nihilistic listlessness that Nietzsche abhors; and opportunity, as it is precisely *because* there is no objective source of meaning that humans depend on that humans have the chance to depend upon *themselves* as sources for meaning and value. But more on this in the next section.

Chapter 4: Nietzsche's Morality – Perspectivism

In the previous section, we covered Nietzsche's views that with the decline of Christianity, Europe was losing its source for an objective set of values—indeed, it was losing objective truth itself. However, this does not mean that Nietzsche was a nihilist; he believed that with the death of God, humanity could make *their own* values. To understand what he meant by this, we have to consider Nietzsche's philosophical view of *perspectivism*.

First, a little background. We all have different experiences of the world, and we see it in different, often contradictory ways. Therefore, a central task for many throughout history, both philosophers and scientists, has been to try to discover facts of the world untainted by any one particular perspective. After all, the logic goes, something that's "true for me" isn't *really* truth; actual truth has to be true for *everyone*. The extremely influential German philosopher Immanuel Kant called this the "thing in itself"—the object not as it's *perceived* to be but as it actually *is*. This view, that there is some facts about the world that are true regardless of one's individual perspective, can safely be called *objectivism*. It is very intuitive, and most readers likely believe in it.

Perspectivism, as might be guessed by the name, is diametrically opposed to this belief system. According to Nietzsche, there is *no such thing* as the thing in itself, there is no "empty point" from which one can view the world without being influenced by any particular perspective. Rather, it's the perspectives *themselves* that create truth, value, and meaning. In other words, it is only within a particular ideology, only within a particular system of beliefs, that truth, meaning, and value are possible. Even if it were possible to extricate oneself entirely from an individual perspective, and Nietzsche does not believe this is possible, all you would achieve is losing any concept of truth altogether.

This might sound depressing, but it's important to keep perspectivism in context with the rest of Nietzsche's arguments. Recall that he *already thinks* that with the decline of Christianity, Europe is losing belief in objective truth and meaning. The alternative to perspectivism is not belief in objective values, because he thought that the death of God made that stance completely untenable. Rather, to him, the alternative to perspectivism was *nihilism*.

Nietzsche agrees with the nihilists that there's no such thing as objective value, meaning, or even truth. Where they disagree is where humans should go from there. According to nihilism, the world is completely empty of meaning and value and so everything humans do is pointless. Perspectivism is as opposed to this viewpoint as it is to objective truth. Certainly, there's no truth or meaning outside of a particular perspective, but that doesn't mean there's *no* truth or meaning. Indeed, as far as Nietzsche is concerned, perspectivism has the potential to be far more life-affirming than Christianity and objective values ever were.

Consider: every person and belief system wants to impose itself on others (more of this in the next section when we talk about the will to power). Christianity just happened to be one of the most successful belief systems in history, imposing itself on over much of the world. But if you grow up just believing in the "objective" truth and values of Christianity, you're not actually *choosing* anything for yourself. Rather, you're almost like a slave, to state it provocatively, following the dictates of another's will until the day you die.

Nietzsche sees perspectivism as having the potential to be life-affirming. Since all of truth and meaning simply come from particular perspectives, that means that by creating a perspective, humans are *themselves* creating truth and meaning. Instead of just passively seeking out "objective" values and accepting them meekly, the duty of humanity becomes to *make its own* values. Subjective meaning is no worse than objective meaning. On the contrary, it could be far better. After all, do you really want to follow a meaning and value system dictated by another, even if that force is God or the "objective" universe itself? And even if you don't believe that, the search for objective value and truth is hopeless. Rather than descending into the melancholic mire of nihilism, perspectivism is the next best thing.

One last thing to note before we move onto the next section: Nietzsche's denial of objective truth might seem self-contradictory, given that he also makes many statements that he seems to suggest are objectively true, such as the master morality/slave morality distinction made earlier or the will to power that will be discussed in the next section. If truth arises only out of a particular perspective, how can Nietzsche assert that any of his other beliefs are true?

This is a major issue in Nietzsche scholarship. As with so many other things, it depends on one's interpretation of Nietzsche. Here's one possible answer, though. With perspectivism, Nietzsche is not denying the existence of truth *altogether*, merely the existence of a truth aside from a particular perspective. So when he talks about things like master morality and slave morality, or the will to power, he's not saying they are true objectively. Rather, he's laying out the perspective *he's* coming from, and he's trying to convince the reader to adopt his perspective as their own. After all, even with perspectivism, one does not lose the ability to judge beliefs or perspectives—beliefs can still be inconsistent with the perspective they arise from, and perspectives can be more or less useful, enjoyable, or as we'll see later, aesthetically pleasing (the standard with which Nietzsche ultimately wants to replace objective morality). And if you accept Nietzsche's perspective, the other assertions he makes will become true for you, absolutely if not objectively.

Chapter 5: Nietzsche and Aesthetics

In the last section we discussed perspectivism, Nietzsche's theory that there are no objective standards for truth or morality, though that doesn't leave out *subjective* standards. In this section, we will discuss what can safely be said to be Nietzsche's standard for evaluating claims of truth and goodness: *aesthetics*.

First, it is apparent from very early on in Nietzsche's writings that he values aesthetics over reason—or at least that he thinks the latter has become too dominant in Western culture. In one of his first books, *The Birth of Tragedy*, he juxtaposes what he calls the "Apollonian" and "Dionysian" worldviews. (Though he didn't develop these terms himself, he certainly popularized them.) Apollo and Dionysus are Greek gods. Most relevantly to our purposes Apollo was the god of reason and Dionysus the god of instincts and ecstasy (as well as wine, which is appropriate). Thus, the Apollonian worldview is one of structure, logic, and order—one that upholds mastering one's emotions and instincts. By contrast, the Dionysian worldview revels in one's emotions, advocating giving oneself over to one's instincts in order to achieve happiness.

Nietzsche argues that the ancient Greeks were primarily Dionysian or at least had a healthy balance between the two ideologies. He blames Socrates for causing the Apollonian worldview to begin taking dominance. Ever since Socrates, Nietzsche says, Western culture has had an unhealthy focus on reason and logic, a turning away from one's emotions and instincts and hence away from one's true self. One can safely say that Nietzsche views this unbalanced subordination of the Dionysian worldview as one of the major factors in Western civilization's slow downfall (along with the victory of slave morality).

One of the results of rejecting the Dionysian worldview is rejecting art altogether. After all, the Apollonian view values truth over all else, and art is essentially a falsehood. By contrast, the Dionysian view is inherently creative and emotional, both of which lie at the core of art. So although Nietzsche thinks that the best works of art combine *both* the Apollonian *and* the Dionysian ideologies (among which he counts some of the Greek tragedies), the ultimate source of art is clearly Dionysian. Because of this, he endows art with all the virtues of the Dionysian worldview, including putting us in touch with our true selves and emotions.

As his philosophy develops, Nietzsche gives art even more importance. He considers art "as the single superior counterforce against all will to negation of life, art as the anti-Christian, anti-Buddhist, anti-Nihilist par excellence". In other words, art is the greatest *promoter* of life in human experience. The reasons for this are somewhat unclear (not uncommon with Nietzsche) but might perhaps be traced back to its connection with the emotions. Emotion and passion, it could be said, lie at the root of life and the human condition. Thus by expressing them, art celebrates life itself. Nietzsche even goes so far as to say that art is the highest activity in which humans can engage.

Why does Nietzsche value art so highly? This gets into areas thorny with controversial interpretations, but a good candidate can be found in Nietzsche's perspectivism worldview as expounded in the previous section. Because the universe has no meaning, order, or truth in and of itself, it is *humans* who are the source of all those things. Humans are the ones who impose morality and value onto a formless universe. But science and rationality assume truth exists "out there" and seeks to *discover* it rather than *create* it. Indeed, one doesn't have to be Nietzsche to agree that science does not deal with "should", it deals with "is". So reason, and the entire Apollonian worldview, is useless for Nietzsche's ultimate quest to reinvent all values.

Instead, it is through art that humanity imposes itself on the world. It is through art that humanity grants meaning to the world. Thus, in the truth-less universe that perspectivism forces upon us, art is the proverbial single shining light in the darkness. If there is no objective morality or truth, as Nietzsche believes, then the only reliable standard that can be used for judgment is aesthetics. If art is the sole celebrator of life, the only source of meaning, then nothing *but* art can be used to decide which values to adopt. And thus, it is through aesthetics that Nietzsche receives his salvation from nihilism. Instead of his perspectivism forcing him to retreat into despair and hopelessness, Nietzsche uses it to cut away what he feels to be all the false and degenerative standards like morality and truth—and the way he does this is by relying on art. Thus, in the end, Nietzsche believes himself to be promoting the beautiful and denouncing the ugly above all.

In the next section, we will see what Nietzsche believes to be the most beautiful form of human. But before then, let's pause for a bit to analyze his philosophy of art. It seems fairly ridiculous and "out-there" at first glance. But consider: in *The Republic*, Plato, the student of Socrates and likely the most important figure in Western philosophy, would ban art in his ideal state, because it increases the passions and interferes with reason. And it's probably not unreasonable to suggest that the chief reason most people view art (in all its forms—movies and TV shows as well as paintings, plays, etc.) is to feel emotions, strong emotions that one may not be able to feel in everyday life.

Even Nietzsche's strongest claim, that aesthetics should be the standard one uses to judge systems of value, may not be as crazy as it first appears. After all, don't we all feel emotionally moved by acts of heroism and emotionally appalled by acts of villainy? Could it not be said that a self-sacrificing saint is more aesthetically pleasing than a self-centered sociopath? Nietzsche's views on what the most aesthetically pleasing form of human life is are certainly controversial, but it's worth considering whether his many critics are taking issue because the Übermensch is opposed to objective morality or because in the end they are emotionally disgusted by the concept.

Chapter 6: Nietzsche's Ideal – The Übermensch

At this point, we have laid enough groundwork that we can finally talk about one of the most important, as well as the most notorious, aspects of Nietzsche's philosophy: the Übermensch, or the overman. This is a better translation than the popularly-conceived one of "superman", so we will use "Übermensch" to avoid possible misconceptions).

Before exploring what the Übermensch *is*, it's important to discuss what it *isn't*. Partly because of Nietzsche's sister, who was a Nazi, the Übermensch is one part of Nietzsche's philosophy that Hitler and the Nazis tried with great gusto to appropriate. They tried to make it be about race: the Aryans were the supermen, or the superior race, and thus had the right to dominate the "inferior races". However, none of this had any basis whatsoever in Nietzsche's thought. Nietzsche was no democrat, a fact that will become clear shortly, but his concept of the Übermensch has nothing whatsoever to do with race.

So what does the Übermensch describe? That is actually an extremely difficult question to answer. Nietzsche's philosophy in general is fairly obscure, as has already been stated, and open to multiple interpretations. Of all his main concepts, only eternal recurrence (which will be discussed in the final section) has less philosophical consensus than the Übermensch. That said, there are some points that most everyone can agree on.

First of all, Nietzsche clearly contradicts the notion of the Übermensch with the notion of the last man, so it would be wise to discuss the Last man first. The last man embodied one possible response to the death of God, and the response that Nietzsche feared was becoming widespread in Western society.

Essentially, the last man is totally apathetic. Faced with a Godless universe devoid of objective truth, the last man decided to not care about anyone or anything. He lacks passion and desire, and he is unwilling to take risks; all he wants is to be safe and comfortable. He makes money only so that he can eat and keep warm. Essentially, he lives for the sake of living, which ironically means that he isn't really living at all—he's like a zombie, even if he does have a pulse. Not surprisingly, this makes him tired of life in general, but he's too much of a coward to commit suicide. In the end, he dies having lived a pointless, meager existence.

The Übermensch, naturally, is the polar opposite of the last man. He too realizes that God is dead and there are no objective values. However, rather than use that as a cause of apathy, he uses it as a cause for celebration. The Übermensch *creates his own* values. He is strong and active; instead of just standing around, he *acts*, forming the world as he goes. Instead of being tired of life, he loves life—not just *living*, or meting out a bleak existence, but life in all its flowering glory. Instead of the last man, who lives as if he's dead, the Übermensch is full of life even if he ends up dying.

This all sounds wonderful, but Nietzsche's Übermensch has a darker side as well—or at least, a side that modern morality (which Nietzsche himself derides as "slave morality") would consider to be darker. While the Übermensch might have a love of "life", that doesn't mean he has a love for individual lives. Indeed, Nietzsche most likely considered the vast majority of peoples' lives to be worthless. He states that an Übermensch would be perfectly willing to sacrifice a great many lives of "lesser" people for his values. Again, the Übermensch is (most likely) not supposed to be *genetically* superior to ordinary people. However, by living a life of meaning in which he creates his own values, his life is *worth* so much more than people who just, last man-style, eke out a miserable existence that Nietzsche thinks he can basically do whatever he wants and would be completely justified in doing so. Indeed, because the Übermensch is creating his own values, literally *nothing* he does can be unjustified (unless, of course, it contradicts with the values he himself sets up).

While further interpretations than this are likely to be very controversial, one thing that can be said is that the Übermensch is most likely the full realization of Nietzsche's views on perspectivism as developed through the death of God and the master/slave morality distinction. His views on the Übermensch being active, strong, and full of the love for life clearly recall his description of the master morality, and his upholding of the Übermensch as the creator of his own values shows that he is the embodiment of all the positive aspects of perspectivism. Put simply, the Übermensch is what Nietzsche wants humanity to become in a Godless universe.

Precisely *why* Nietzsche wants humanity to become Übermenschen is an interesting question in itself. Because of his perspectivism, he clearly can't base it on some kind of objective moral standard or he would be contradicting himself. Rather, Nietzsche seems to favor the Übermensch because he is *aesthetically* superior to the good Christian who (in Nietzsche's view) blindly accepts the dictates of the Church, or the last man who lives life comfortably and listlessly. It's as if all the world were a stage, as Shakespeare put it, and the Übermensch are the only characters worth watching. So the Übermensch can also be seen as Nietzsche's way of replacing morality with aesthetics and urging humanity to live not for happiness, or brute comfort, but rather in the most beautiful way they can—in all senses of the word "beautiful".

Now, at this point you may still be unconvinced. You may think that in the end, Nietzsche was really just providing a formula for tyrants to justify their behavior to themselves, and maybe he wasn't so far removed from the Nazis after all. That is an interpretation many readers of Nietzsche have, and it may not be wrong. But consider: Nietzsche is by no means the only person to worry about human society devolving into a last man-type state, even if not everybody uses those words. Thinkers from all over the political spectrum have worried that humans are becoming more and more concerned with base comfort and brute survival, refraining from taking any risks whatsoever, caring about continuing to exist so much that they forget to live. The theme of the average person working so they can eat so they can work has practically become a cliché. The solution might not be an Übermensch-type figure who creates his or her own values and is accountable to no one but himself or herself. However, in your rush to condemn Nietzsche's solution, don't lose sight of the problem he was trying to solve.

Chapter 7: Nietzsche on Politics and Self-Improvement

The previous sections of this article offered a natural progression, from master/slave morality to the death of God to perspectivism to aesthetics to the fulfillment of all those ideas, the Übermensch. In this last part of the article, we will discuss some other aspects of Nietzsche's philosophy that, while certainly connected with the previous concepts, still stand somewhat independently. In this section we will discuss Nietzsche's political philosophy (or, perhaps more appropriately, his anti-political philosophy) and his ideas for what people should do to improve themselves. We will then move on to the will to power in the next section, and finish up with perhaps the strangest concept in all of Nietzsche's works, the eternal recurrence.

So what is Nietzsche's political philosophy? Perhaps surprisingly to those who think he's a totalitarian, or maybe an anarchist, to a large extent Nietzsche did not *have* a political philosophy. He does occasionally say very negative things about the state, that it's "the coldest of all cold monsters" and "everything about it is false"—but those are passing remarks more than anything else, and he certainly never forms any sort of coherent alternative to the state. And one could perhaps make the argument that Nietzsche's Übermensch, should he ever come to exist, would deserve to rule over everyone else in a totalitarian manner, though again Nietzsche doesn't ever actually state that.

Something that Nietzsche *does* state is an unequivocal elitism. He consistently denigrates the majority of humanity as "the herd" or "the rabble" and makes it clear he has no concern whatsoever for them. In *The Antichrist*, he says that "This book belongs to the very few" and says that it's not a problem if a book is impossible to understand because "perhaps that was part of the author's intention—he did not want to be understood by just 'anybody.'" And as was discussed in the previous section, he thinks the Übermensch has the right to do whatever he wants with the mass of humanity that does not have the ability to become as great as him. However, this does not necessarily have any implications for a *political* one. Indeed, Nietzsche tends to express an explicitly *anti*-political view more often than not.

What does that mean? In *Thus Spoke Zarathustra*, Nietzsche states that "Only where the state ends, there begins the human being who is not superfluous." This non-superfluous human is one who values solitude: "Far from the market place and from fame happens all that is great." In other words, anyone who spends all or most of their time in a public life, whether that be as an agent of the state or even as a worker in a corporation, is essentially living a superfluous life. It is only if one shuts themselves off from society and works in solitude—probably not coincidentally, if one lives a life much like Nietzsche's himself—that one can become great.

This seems odd at first glance. Doesn't Nietzsche think that powerful political figures, or rich business leaders, are great? But recall in the section on aesthetics that Nietzsche thinks that *art* is the highest possible accomplishment of mankind. He would definitely not be the first to notice that the great artists are often the most reclusive, spending days by themselves creating their works. This focus on art and the act of creating may also explain his prescription for what people should do to become great:

the dangerousness of [man's] situation must first grow to the point of enormity, his power of invention and simulation (his "spirit") had to develop under prolonged pressure and constraint into refinement and audacity.

He also says of the people he is most concerned with:

> I wish [them] suffering, desolation, sickness, ill-treatment, indignities—I wish that they should not remain unfamiliar with profound self-contempt, the torture of self-mistrust, the wretchedness of the vanquished.

Essentially, Nietzsche is saying that you have to suffer, to feel pain, to be in danger, in order to become great. It should perhaps be noted here that the famous quote "What doesn't kill me makes me stronger" in fact originates with Nietzsche. He thinks that pain and suffering are necessary for humanity to reach its full potential—which, incidentally, is another reason he despises most of modern humanity, for he thinks the vast majority of human beings are content just to seek out pleasure and avoid pain, not caring about becoming great.

But none of this adds up to any kind of *political* program. He never states that his reclusive artist ideal should end up ruling over the rest of humanity. Indeed, it seems clear that his ideal *cannot* rule, as whatever else a totalitarian dictator is, he certainly isn't reclusive. And while Nietzsche does criticize the state, he doesn't do it in order to advocate tearing it down or even improving it; he does it to encourage people to *avoid* the state, to avoid politics altogether.

Above, it was stated that Nietzsche is an anti-political thinker. This is because he thinks that the public sphere does nothing but ruin the potential of the few humans who have the ability to become truly great, to become Übermenschen. His moral philosophy is explicitly addressed to the individual—to a very small number of individuals, actually—and he cares not at all what the mass of humanity chooses to do with its politics and economics. They are just superfluous, "the herd", and all Nietzsche wants of them is to stay out of the way of the ones who are actually worth something.

All this has perhaps painted a too-negative view of Nietzsche's views. Certainly, it's hard to sugar-coat his extreme elitism, which is both blatant and widespread—the reader must simply take it or leave it. But Nietzsche is not the only one to worry that a preoccupation with happiness and an aversion to pain interferes with the creative potential of humanity. And he is certainly *not* the only one to feel that spending one's life in politics or the marketplace has nothing but a deleterious impact on one's character. After all, one might argue, if you spend all your time trying to win people's votes or their money, aren't you ultimately just depending upon others for your self-worth and your happiness? Is that really a healthy way to live? Maybe some solitude really is necessary for the human spirit to flourish, though most will not wish to take this concept to the extremes that Nietzsche does. Of course, that's true with the vast majority of Nietzsche's theories.

Chapter 8: Nietzsche on Psychology – The Will to Power

A somewhat common theme throughout philosophical history has been what the root basis of all human action is. The problem essentially goes like this: most of what humans do, we do for some purpose other than the act itself. For example, we work in order to make money, we make money in order to eat food, we eat food in order to survive (or, perhaps, to gain pleasure from the eating), and so on. Clearly, though, there have to be *some* acts that don't fit this pattern, some acts that we do for themselves and not for any other reason—otherwise, our motivations would spiral backward into infinity. There could be multiple such motivations, of course, but it's prettier if one's theory can reduce all of human action to one basic motivation.

For example, one classic view is that all human action is ultimately in order to get *happiness*. The theory goes that happiness is the one thing that humans want in and of itself; we never want to be happy so that we can be something else, we want to be happy so that we can be happy. There are other theories as well. Arthur Schopenhauer, who was a heavy influence on Nietzsche in many ways, theorized that all action—not just human—comes from a "will to live," and so living is the one thing that creatures desire in and of itself.

Nietzsche explicitly rejects these views. He thinks that the basic desire of all living creatures is not happiness, life, or anything else, but *power*. Power is the one thing we want for itself; everything else is just a means to that end.

This may seem implausible at first blush, but it's important to note that Nietzsche means something quite general by "power". Essentially, what he's talking about is the ability to control the external world. Consider, for example, "locked-in syndrome": the disease in which one is conscious but trapped in one's own body, unable to make any movement whatsoever. Nietzsche would say this is horrifying to us because our power over our own bodies is one of the most basic powers there is. With barely a thought, we can make our bodies move however we want them to. While we gain very little pleasure from it normally, locked-in syndrome, by removing our entire ability to influence the outside world, makes humans' existence so miserable that most people would rather die than suffer it.

One can think of the will to power as taking this insight and expanding it to the domain of the entirety of human action. Physical strength and political authority are certainly manifestations of the will to power, and Nietzsche would explain both in terms of that principle, but they are not the only ones or even, perhaps, the most common ones. Indeed, Nietzsche thinks one of the benefits of his theory is that it can even explain actions such as asceticism, or renouncing the world completely and living in isolation. He would say those arise in realization of the little influence one often has over the political world, and the comparatively massive influence one can have over a world of one's own making.

He also thinks reducing human motivation to power, as opposed to happiness or life, explains actions such as warriors willing to die for glory or victory. It is hard to explain how a desire for either of the above two could motivate something like this. However, the will to power can explain it quite easily: what those warriors want is power, power over their enemies, and they'd rather die than lose it.

At some points, Nietzsche even seems to extend the will to power to cover, not just human psychology, but the nature of the entire universe. He sometimes seems to suggest that matter itself always moves for the purpose of gaining power for itself. For example, one could view gravity as the result of lumps of mass trying to exert their influence over each other. Since Nietzsche was not a fan of substances or essences, he might even have been suggesting that power was the basic entity of the entire universe, underlying everything else, all matter and energy. However, this view is very controversial in Nietzsche scholarship; many think that, overall, he mostly intended for the will to power to be a psychological theory.

The reader is likely still skeptical at this stage, and perhaps rightly so. It is, perhaps, right to say that human motivation is so complex and variable that any attempt to narrow it down to one underlying purpose is doomed to fail from the start. But in an age where we tend to assume that people are acting mainly to be happy or to have as much pleasure as they can, the will to power might serve as a useful antidote. Consider why we're so horrified by locked-in syndrome, why we're so repulsed by mental disorders that leave people unable to control even their own minds, and why so many are willing to die for so many (seemingly) different reasons.

Reducing everything to the desire for power might seem cynical, but it might be safe to say that Nietzsche took it in an almost idealistic way. To end this section, ruminate on the following passage from Nietzsche's notebooks, one of the best for showing the almost romantic regard he had for what he took to be "power":

I have found strength where one does not look for it: in simple, mild, and pleasant people, without the least desire to rule—and, conversely, the desire to rule has often appeared to me a sign of inward weakness: they fear their own slave soul and shroud it in a royal cloak (in the end, they still become the slaves of their followers, their fame, etc.). The powerful natures dominate, it is a necessity, they need not lift one finger.

Chapter 9: Nietzsche and the Eternal Recurrence

As has been stated numerous times, Nietzsche is famous for being difficult to understand and open to many possible interpretations. However, even in that context, the eternal recurrence (also known as the "eternal return") stands out as being particularly obscure. While the concept enough is easy enough to understand, if not appreciate, the precise role it plays in Nietzsche's overall outlook is extremely unclear. This article will not attempt to offer solutions to this problem; instead, it will lay out the problem and let the reader make up their own mind.

But enough beating around the bush. The reader probably knows of the Big Bang theory. There is also a theory called the "Big Crunch"—that at some point, the entire universe will collapse back into a singularity, and then another Big Bang will happen, creating a new universe. That theory goes on to state that similar cycles of Big Bangs and Big Crunches have happened an infinite number of times already, and will happen an infinite number of times in the future.

Now, imagine that in one of those previous universes, everything that happened in this universe occurred. Your life, the life of everyone you know and has ever been, *will* ever be, the entire history of the universe, already happened in a previous universe. In addition, imagine that in a future universe, everything will happen once again. Nothing is unique—it all already happened an infinite number of times and will happen again an infinite number of times.

That's eternal recurrence.

At this point, ask yourself: if you found out eternal recurrence was true, that everything that is once was and will be again, what would your reaction be? Would you be filled with an unaccountable dread and lock yourself in your room, unable to stand reality? Or would you fall on your knees and thank the heavens for making such a wonderful world as this?

It seems like a ridiculous question. Setting aside the intentional hyperbole in describing the reaction in an extreme manner, it is true that most people have a very negative reaction to the prospect of eternal recurrence. For some reason, it seems like a very disturbing idea, and most would be quite depressed if it was actually true (though they might not lock themselves in their rooms). But why is the prospect of eternal recurrence so horrifying to us?

Nietzsche actually puts more weight on the *reaction* people have to eternal recurrence than the theory itself. Indeed, many Nietzsche scholars think that eternal recurrence is just a thought experiment, and Nietzsche did not actually believe it was true. Setting aside that issue, Nietzsche believes that one should feel *joy* at the prospect of eternal recurrence. Actually, that's underselling it: Nietzsche believes that *wanting* eternal recurrence to be true is the mark of true greatness, that it's the only way one can achieve a true love of life.

This is a very odd position. Explaining it has been the task of Nietzsche scholars for decades, and they have not succeeded—hence, why this concept is so obscure. This article will provide a basic way of thinking about the problem.

Eternal recurrence is linked with the idea of *amor fati*. This is Latin for "love of fate", and it seems to be central to Nietzsche's conception of what the ideal outlook on life is. Essentially, Nietzsche wants people to accept the world *in its totality*. Most people would agree that, while there is much good in this world, there is much evil as well. But Nietzsche loves both the good *and* the evil. He loves the beautiful and the ugly; indeed, in the end, the ugly may be the most beautiful of all. To Nietzsche, accepting eternal recurrence is to have *amor fati*, and that's to not want anything to be different, to accept the world just as it is and *love* it for it.

With this in mind, it perhaps becomes clearer what Nietzsche means when he says that accepting eternal recurrence is necessary to have a true love of life (though, like almost everything else in this article, this is bound to be controversial). There are many good parts to life, but there are many bad parts as well. There is happiness, but also misery; pleasure, but also pain; love, but also hatred; friendship, but also loneliness. To live means to feel joy, but it also means to feel sadness. Therefore, to state that you love life but hate pain is a contradiction in terms. Life *is* pain, and misery, and sadness, as well as happiness and all the other so-called "good" things. Idealists want to take away the bad and leave only the good, but in the end, maybe all that would accomplish would be getting rid of life itself. To love life means to accept it, *all* of it, and not want it to be different. And to accept eternal recurrence, even to wish for it, is to love the world so much that you'd be happy if it all happened in exactly the same way.

To a modern reader, or even one of Nietzsche's day, the above-stated view might seem perverse. Surely, Nietzsche isn't saying that the world is perfect as it is? Surely, he isn't saying that there's no point in trying to make the world a better place—that attempting to improve matters is only revealing an inner hatred of life? An objector might argue that Nietzsche had argued in favor of an Übermensch who created his own values and reformed the world in his image—does that mean the Übermensch doesn't love life? Indeed, isn't acting *at all* an attempt to remake the world in a manner more to one's liking; isn't that the entire point of Nietzsche's vaunted will to power? How can he possibly state that one should just accept the world as it is, with all its pain, misery, and horror?

Perhaps Nietzsche really is saying something perverse, and maybe he really is contradicting himself. It wouldn't be the first time he did either. But when a man as brilliant as Nietzsche undoubtedly was places so much importance on something, it would be a good idea to take a second look before rejecting it altogether. Certainly, few would deny that we should try to make the world a better place. But life isn't all happiness and mirth, and maybe, in the end, it is good that it's not. Pain is important, and so is misery. On the scale of something like the Holocaust, or even an average run-of-the-mill murder, pain turns into something undesirable; but in moderation, it might be a good thing. Perhaps we shouldn't accept eternal recurrence with open arms—but on our deathbed, don't we all want to be satisfied with the life we live and not be willing to trade it for another, even if it contained vast amounts of pain and suffering?

Or maybe all the above is wrong, just the pretentious, naïve assertions of a sheltered life who never got to know true suffering. Then again, while one can say many things about Nietzsche, "he never knew true suffering" is likely not one of the. So it is worth considering, at least.

Conclusion: Nietzsche's Legacy

This article has just scratched the surface of Nietzsche's philosophy. The number of books that could be—indeed, that *have* been—written about him could fill several libraries. He has influenced people as diverse as Hannah Arendt and Ayn Rand. While this article could not hope to cover all that is worth covering in Nietzsche's works, it hopefully has shown you why he has been fascinating to so many people over the last century, and most likely the centuries to come. Even if one disagrees with him, one cannot just disregard him. Friedrich Wilhelm Nietzsche was a complicated man, a brilliant philosopher—and perhaps, above all else (which he might have taken to be the greatest of compliments), a phenomenal writer. If the reader wants to learn more about him, there is no better way than picking up one of his books and reading it. At the very least, it will not be a boring ride.

About the Publisher

BookCaps™ is building a library of low cost study guides; if you enjoyed this book, look for other books in the "Plain and Simple English" series at **www.bookcaps.com**.

3214308R00022

Printed in Great Britain
by Amazon.co.uk, Ltd.,
Marston Gate.